HORSES

The CLYDESDALE Horse

by John Diedrich

Consultant:
Martin E. English, DVM
President, Clydesdale Breeders of the U.S.A.
Pecatonica, Illinois

press

Mankato, Minnesota

Edge Books are published by Capstone Press,
151 Good Counsel Drive, P.O. Box 669, Mankato, Minnesota 56002.
www.capstonepress.com

Library of Congress Cataloging-in-Publication Data
Diedrich, John.
  The Clydesdale horse / by John Diedrich.
    p. cm.—(Edge books. Horses)
  Includes bibliographical references (p. 31) and index.
  ISBN 0-7368-3766-3 (hardcover)
  1. Clydesdale horse—Juvenile literature. I. Title. II. Series.
SF293.C65D54 2005
636.1'5—dc22   2004019417

Summary: Describes Clydesdale horses, including their history, physical features,
and primary uses.

Editorial Credits
Angie Kaelberer, editor; Juliette Peters, designer; Deirdre Barton,
    photo researcher; Scott Thoms, photo editor

Photo Credits
Capstone Press/Gary Sundermeyer, 7, 21; Juliette Peters, 20
Corbis/Kelly-Mooney Photography, 16–17
Gloria Muscarella/Cheval Photography, 5, 8, 11, 13, 23, 27, 29
Karen Patterson, 22
© 2004 Mark J. Barrett, cover, back cover, 12, 25
Pam Mackenzie, 6, 14, 19

**For more information about Clydesdales, contact the Clydesdale Breeders
of the U.S.A. at 17346 Kelley Road, Pecatonica, Illinois 61063, or visit
http://www.clydesusa.com.**

1 2 3 4 5 6 10 09 08 07 06 05

Table of Contents

Chapter 1

Willing Workers

The Clydesdale is one of the most familiar horse breeds. Most people have seen the large, strong Clydesdales in TV commercials, movies, and magazines.

The Clydesdale belongs to a group called draft horses. These strong horses were first bred to work on farms and to pull large loads in cities. They are still used for these purposes in some parts of the world.

Beginning of the Breed

The Clydesdale breed began in the early 1700s in a part of Scotland called Lanarkshire. Lanarkshire is near the large city of Glasgow.

Learn about:
- ★ Draft horses
- ★ Clydesdale history
- ★ Growth of the breed

Clydesdales are draft horses.
They were first bred for farm work
and to pull carts and wagons.

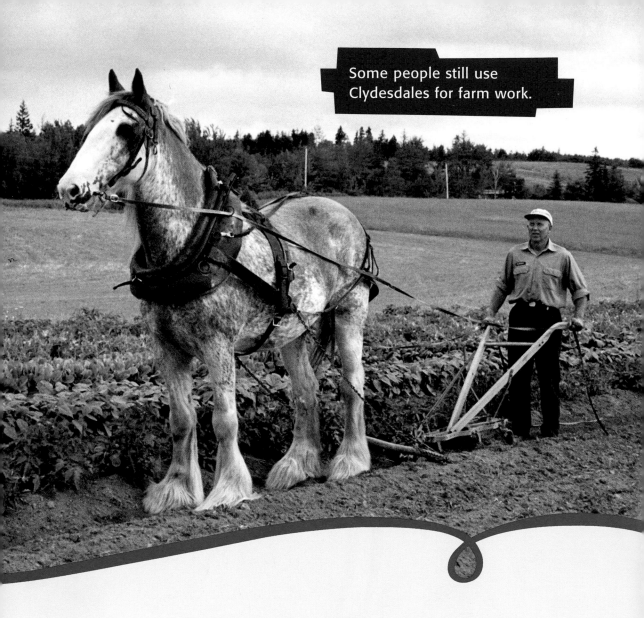

Some people still use Clydesdales for farm work.

Glasgow was near coalfields. The coal workers needed strong horses to pull the heavy coal wagons. As Scotland's cities grew, so did the need for coal. The coal workers needed stronger and faster horses to keep up with the demand.

Around 1720, a Lanarkshire farmer named John Patterson bought a large black Flemish stallion in England. He bred the stallion to the smaller Scottish mares. The mares' foals were the earliest ancestors of today's Clydesdales.

Lanarkshire farmers continued to breed the large horses. Over time, the farmers produced a powerful horse with a long stride. Farmers hitched the horses to plows to work their fields. The farmers called the horses Clydesdales. Lanarkshire is in the dale, or valley, of the Clyde River.

World Travelers

In 1826, Clydesdale owners showed off their horses at a world's fair called the Glasgow Exhibition. There, people from around the world saw Clydesdales for the first time.

Word spread about the big Scottish draft horses. People from other countries came to Scotland to buy Clydesdales. The new owners took the horses back to their own countries.

Today, Clydesdales often pull wagons at parades and festivals.

By the late 1800s, the Clydesdale breed had spread to North America. There, Clydesdales were used for farm work and to pull large loads in cities. In 1910, about 16,000 Clydesdales lived in the United States.

Years of Decline

By the 1930s, people needed fewer horses for work. Farmers replaced horses with tractors and other farm machines. Cars replaced horse-drawn carriages and wagons.

Clydesdale numbers decreased for the next 30 years. The breed was in danger of dying out.

Recent Years

In the 1960s, more people began raising Clydesdales. This time, the horses were bred as show horses as well as for farm work. More Clydesdale shows and sales were held as people became interested in the big, gentle horses.

Today, about 6,000 Clydesdales live in the United States. The Clydesdale Breeders of the U.S.A. keeps track of each U.S. Clydesdale's ancestry. This group formed in 1879.

Chapter 2

Gentle Giants

Clydesdales are born big. A newborn Clydesdale foal weighs about 125 to 150 pounds (57 to 68 kilograms).

A horse's height is measured in hands. A hand equals 4 inches (10 centimeters). An adult Arabian horse is 14 to 15 hands tall at the withers, or the top of the shoulders. The average Clydesdale reaches this height by its first birthday.

Most Clydesdales reach their full height of 16 to 19 hands by age 3 or 4. Adult Clydesdales weigh between 1,600 and 2,300 pounds (725 and 1,050 kilograms). They are as heavy as small cars.

Learn about:
★ Size
★ Appearance
★ Temperament

A newborn Clydesdale weighs as much as an average woman.

Features

The Clydesdale has more refined features than most draft breeds. Clydesdales have longer legs and more streamlined bodies. They also have a high-stepping trot.

▼ Most Clydesdales have white markings.

The Clydesdale's lower legs are covered in long, silky hair called feather. The feather flows in the air as the Clydesdale trots.

The Clydesdale's hooves are larger than those of most other breeds. Each hoof is about the size of a large dinner plate.

Color

Clydesdales can be one of several colors. Bay is the most common color pattern. Bay horses are red-brown with a black mane and tail. Clydesdales can also be brown, black, chestnut, or roan. Chestnut is a shade of copper or red. Roan Clydesdales have coats of one solid color mixed with white hairs.

Most Clydesdales have white markings. A Clydesdale may have a white stripe called a blaze on its face. If the whole face is white, it is called a bald face. White markings on the lower legs are called socks or stockings. Some Clydesdales have white patches on their bodies.

FACT

A large adult Clydesdale's withers are above a 6-foot (1.8-meter) person's head.

Personality

Clydesdales are gentle and cooperative. They work hard and seem to want to please their owners. Their personalities make them easy to train.

Gentleness and cooperation are good characteristics for any horse. They are especially important for the big, powerful Clydesdale. A 2,000-pound (900-kilogram) horse with poor manners could be dangerous to people and other horses.

◀ Clydesdales' gentle, cooperative personalities make them good show horses for young people.

Bald face

Wide nostrils

Deep, wide chest

White stockings

Withers

Short, broad back

Long hind legs

Feather

Chapter 3

Champions in Harness

Today, few Clydesdales are used for farm work. But many owners still train their Clydesdales to pull wagons. A Clydesdale can pull a wagon alone or with a team of horses.

Learning to Pull

People start training their Clydesdales to pull wagons when the horses are about 2 years old. The trainer uses a harness and bridle to train the Clydesdale. The harness connects the horse to the wagon. The bridle holds a metal piece called a bit in the horse's mouth. The bit is attached to the lines. The driver uses the lines to steer.

Learn about:
- ★ Training
- ★ Hitch competitions
- ★ Shows

Clydesdales sometimes pull sleighs through deep snow.

Clydesdales wear harnesses during hitch competitions.

Soon, the young Clydesdale becomes used to the harness and bridle. The trainer hitches the young horse with an older, well-trained horse. The older horse pulls the young horse in the direction that the trainer is steering them.

A Winning Team

Hitches are teams of two, three, four, six, or eight horses harnessed together. Clydesdale hitches are usually made up of horses that are the same size and color. The horses trot together smoothly as they respond to the driver's commands.

Hitch competitions have different classes for the different sizes of hitches. Teams are judged on how well they work together. A good team and trainer make driving look easy. A team must start and stop when asked. A team also should steer easily and turn smoothly.

Major Competitions

The biggest Clydesdale show in the United States is the National Show. This four-day event takes place each August at the Wisconsin State Fair in West Allis. The show

Three Clydesdales make up a unicorn hitch.

GLENVIEW

Clydesdales

includes breed, cart, hitch, and halter classes.

Breed competitions are like beauty or fitness contests. Horses show against other Clydesdales of the same sex and age. The horse that best represents the breed wins.

In halter classes, horses aren't ridden or hitched to a harness. Instead, owners use a halter to lead the horses on foot.

Many state fairs and county fairs hold draft horse shows that include classes for Clydesdales. Young 4-H members often show their Clydesdales at these events. 4-H is an organization that teaches young people about leadership and community service.

⬇ Clydesdales win ribbons at breed competitions.

Chapter 4

Clydesdales in Action

Like all horses, Clydesdales need plenty of room. Many Clydesdale owners live in the country and keep their horses in barns on their property. Clydesdale owners who live in cities pay to board their horses at nearby farms or stables.

Draft horses eat about twice as much as smaller horses eat. Adult Clydesdales need 25 to 50 pounds (11 to 23 kilograms) of hay each day. They also eat about 5 to 10 pounds (2 to 5 kilograms) of concentrated feed daily. This food is made up of grain, vitamins, minerals, and molasses.

Learn about:
- ★ Care
- ★ Hippotherapy
- ★ Anheuser-Busch team

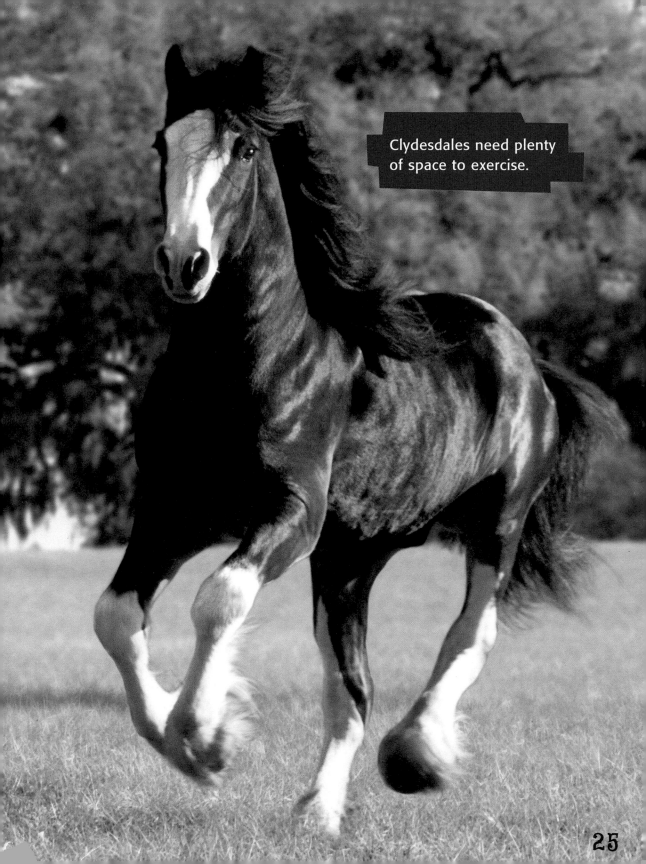

Clydesdales need plenty of space to exercise.

Other Uses

Clydesdale horses are best known for harness and team competitions. But they also make good riding horses. Many people use Clydesdales for trail riding, jumping events, and dressage competitions. In dressage events, horses complete a pattern as they perform a series of advanced moves.

Some people use Clydesdales in hippotherapy programs. Hippotherapy uses riding to treat people who have disabilities. For example, a person who is unable to walk can feel the horse's movements during a ride. Riders can imitate these movements as they try to walk on their own. Clydesdales' calm, hardworking personalities make them good choices for these programs.

Clydesdales are also used for other jobs. They pull carriages at weddings and parades. A few people use them to pull logs in forests.

Clydesdales attract attention wherever they go. These gentle giants continue to amaze people with their strength, beauty, and friendly nature.

Anheuser-Busch Clydesdales

The Anheuser-Busch Company has been famous for its Clydesdale teams since 1933. Today, the company owns six teams of eight Clydesdales. It sends the horses to state fairs, parades, and other events all over North America.

Anheuser-Busch Clydesdales are bay geldings at least 4 years old. They stand 18 hands high and have four white stockings, plus a white blaze on the face.

Each Clydesdale team travels about 10 months of the year. Anheuser-Busch spends about $6,000 per day on each team's care. When not traveling, the horses live on farms or at theme parks owned by Anheuser-Busch.

The Clydesdale Horse

Name: The Clydesdale breed's name comes from the dale, or valley, of the Clyde River in Scotland. Clydesdales were first bred in this valley.

History: The Clydesdale breed began in Scotland in the early 1700s. Flemish stallions were bred to Scottish draft mares.

Height: Clydesdales are 16 to 19 hands (about 6 feet or 1.8 meters) at the withers. Each hand equals 4 inches (10 centimeters).

Weight: 1,600 to 2,300 pounds (725 to 1,050 kilograms)

Colors: bay, brown, black, chestnut, roan

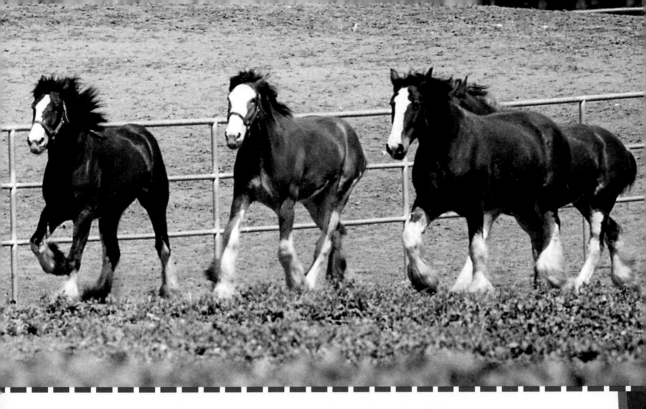

Features: wide foreheads; large eyes; feather on the legs; long stride; high-stepping trot

Abilities: Besides pulling carts and wagons, Clydesdales do well as show horses and in hippotherapy programs. Many people also use them for trail riding, jumping, and dressage.

Personality: gentle, cooperative, hardworking

Life span: 20 to 25 years

Glossary

bridle (BRYE-duhl)—the straps that fit around a horse's head and connect to a bit to control a horse while riding

dressage (druh-SAHJ)—a riding style in which horses complete a pattern while doing advanced moves

gelding (GEL-ding)—an adult male horse that can't be used for breeding

halter (HAWL-tur)—a rope or strap used to lead a horse; the halter fits over the horse's nose and behind its ears.

harness (HAR-niss)—a set of straps and metal pieces that connect a horse to a plow, cart, or wagon

hippotherapy (hip-oh-THAIR-uh-pee)—a treatment that uses horseback riding to help people with disabilities

mare (MAIR)—an adult female horse

stallion (STAL-yuhn)—an adult male horse that can be used for breeding

withers (WITH-urs)—the top of a horse's shoulders; a horse's height is measured from the ground to the withers.

Read More

Dalgleish, Sharon. *Working Horses*. Farm Animals. Philadelphia: Chelsea House, 2005.

Hull, Mary E. *The Horse in Harness*. The Horse Library. Philadelphia: Chelsea House, 2002.

Murray, Julie. *Clydesdale Horses*. Animal Kingdom. Edina, Minn.: Abdo, 2003.

Internet Sites

FactHound offers a safe, fun way to find Internet sites related to this book. All of the sites on FactHound have been researched by our staff.

Here's how:

1. Visit *www.facthound.com*
2. Type in this special code **0736837663** for age-appropriate sites. Or enter a search word related to this book for a more general search.
3. Click on the **Fetch It** button.

FactHound will fetch the best sites for you!

Index